The Big Story

What Being a Journalist Is Really Like

Jim Schembri

Illustrated by Roger Harvey

2000 Barrie Publishing Pty Limited
The Big Story: What Being a Journalist Is Really Like
Text copyright © Jim Schembri
Illustrations copyright © Roger Harvey

Momentum program © Barrie Publishing Pty Limited

Published by Troll Communications L.L.C.
Reprinted by arrangement with Barrie Publishing Pty Limited, 89 High Street, Kew, Australia, 3101

ISBN 0 8167 6815 3

Prepress by Splitting Image Colour Studio Pty Ltd
Printed in Singapore by PH Productions Pte Ltd
10 9 8 7 6 5 4 3 2 1

Every effort has been made to contact the owners of the photographs in this book. Where this has not been possible, we invite the owners of the copyright to notify the publishers.

Pages 31, 32, 33, author photos courtesy of the Age; Corel Photo Studio images 314037, 314043, which are protected under the copyright laws of the U.S., Canada and elsewhere, used under license; cover, title page, 3, 4, 5, 7, 9, 11, 13, 15, 17, 19, 27, 28, 29, 34, 35, 36, 37, 38 (illustrations), Roger Harvey.

Whose messy desk is this?

Hey, that's my desk! Hi. I'm Lauren Trent, and I've just finished writing a big story for tomorrow's newspaper. I'll tell you all about it—and my messy desk!—as soon as I get a bottle of water.

Journalists drink lots of water. We also drink a lot of tea and coffee—probably way too much! Almost every desk you see in this newspaper office has a cup or a bottle on it. That's because we spend so much time at our desks writing stories. You might even see plates and cutlery on some desks, too. Sometimes, we are so busy, we have breakfast, lunch, and even dinner at our desks! That's okay, because we have our own cafeteria right here in the building.

I'm sorry my desk is such a mess. If you are a busy journalist like me, it's hard to keep your desk neat and tidy. All the mail and newspapers and magazines just pile up, and you can't always find time to clean up.

Time is important when you are a journalist. You are always looking for it, have too little of it, or are running out of it. There is never enough of it! To be a good journalist, you must be able to organize your time. You have to think fast and work fast, which is what I did with the story I just finished.

So, what's the big story, Lauren?

The story I wrote today was an interesting one about a pod of whales that swam into the bay early this morning.

When I arrived at work, I had no idea I would be doing this story. That's one of the things that makes being a journalist for a big city newspaper so exciting.

How did you get to do the story?

The news editor of the paper assigned me to cover the story. While driving into work this morning, she heard a report on the radio about a group of whales that was swimming into the bay. She thought it sounded like a good news story for the paper.

She mentioned the story at the morning news conference. A news conference is where the section editors all meet with the executive editor and managing editor. The section editors are in charge of the different sections of the newspaper, such as local news, national news, international news, and sports. They all talk about what is happening, and what should go into the paper the next day.

The executive editor said the whale story sounded great, and that someone should go out with a photographer.

After the news conference, the news editor asked me to cover the whale story. She gave me a few ideas about who I should talk to and some of the questions I should ask. I had my own ideas, too. She assigned a photographer, and I went to work.

What was the first thing you had to do?

It is important to know as much as you can about a story before you go out to cover it. That is, of course, if you have time! So, after the news editor told me about the story, I did some research. I only had about fifteen minutes before the photographer and I had to leave. It's an hour's drive to the coast. We had to hurry, because the whales could have left before we arrived!

Luckily, having computers means you can do your research at your desk. Before computers, journalists had to use the newspaper's library. This involved looking through filing cabinets stuffed full of newspaper clippings. It could take ages!

Today, without leaving my desk, I can use my computer to search many newspapers and magazines for stories about a particular subject in just a few seconds.

For my whale story, I checked for recent articles about whales entering the bay. I found a story, written ten years ago, about a similar thing happening in exactly the same place. One of the whales hit a boat and knocked someone overboard. That was an important piece of information, because it gave me a lead. The man who owned the boat might have some interesting comments for my story. I made a note to try to find him.

9

The Internet can also be useful for research—as long as you don't waste time surfing the net! I was able to get some scientific information about whales and their migration patterns.

Because we were in a hurry, I had to print out all of this material and read it in the car. I was able to use the information when I asked people questions. People always like you to know what you are talking about when you interview them.

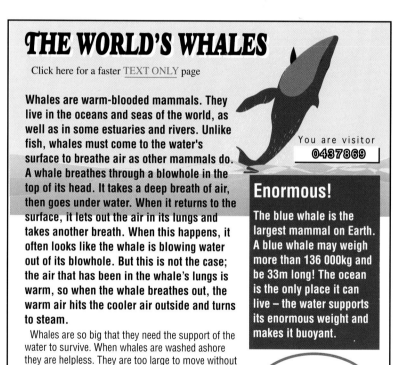

THE WORLD'S WHALES

Click here for a faster TEXT ONLY page

Whales are warm-blooded mammals. They live in the oceans and seas of the world, as well as in some estuaries and rivers. Unlike fish, whales must come to the water's surface to breathe air as other mammals do. A whale breathes through a blowhole in the top of its head. It takes a deep breath of air, then goes under water. When it returns to the surface, it lets out the air in its lungs and takes another breath. When this happens, it often looks like the whale is blowing water out of its blowhole. But this is not the case; the air that has been in the whale's lungs is warm, so when the whale breathes out, the warm air hits the cooler air outside and turns to steam.

Whales are so big that they need the support of the water to survive. When whales are washed ashore they are helpless. They are too large to move without the support of the water, and the huge weight of their body can even crush their lungs and make them unable to breathe. This is why they need the help of humans to return them to the safety of the deep water.

GO! ➡ next page

You are visitor
0437869

Enormous!

The blue whale is the largest mammal on Earth. A blue whale may weigh more than 136 000kg and be 33m long! The ocean is the only place it can live – the water supports its enormous weight and makes it buoyant.

Did you know?
Whales, dolphins and porpoises are the only mammals that live their whole life in the water.

What happened when you arrived at the bay?

When we arrived, the beach was buzzing with people: other journalists and photographers, television crews, local people, sightseers, police and rescue officers. This was obviously a big news story. We were taken out on a police boat to see the whales. The photographer took some beautiful pictures of them as they swam around. We didn't want to get too close, of course, so he used a telephoto lens. I took some notes about the number of whales, their size, and color.

Back on the beach, I interviewed the local police chief about the whales. He told me what time they were first spotted. He explained the hazards they could cause to fishing boats.

After that, I spoke to the person who first spotted the whales this morning. Then I found the man whose boat was hit when whales came into the bay ten years ago. He was stunned that I knew his boat's name!

There were many scientists and marine experts there to see the whales. I interviewed one of them about why the whales had come into the bay. I also asked some local residents what they thought about the whales.

These are what all the fuss is about!

How can you take notes if you are running around so much?

When they start their training, most journalists learn how to use shorthand. This is a way of writing quickly by using little symbols that stand for different words. It is an important skill for every journalist.

Sometimes, however, it is awkward to use shorthand when you are doing a story. Like today; it would have been difficult for me to stand there taking notes on paper while people were talking. One of the reasons was that it started to rain.

These days, most newspaper journalists use tape recorders. This way, you can record the interview on tape and listen to it later. It also means that you can get the quotes exactly right.

So, you gathered all your information. What then?

When I returned to the office, I spoke to the news editor again. She wanted to know if the story was worth including in the paper. I told her it was an interesting story, and we had some great pictures. I also told her that there were other journalists there. This meant that everybody else would be covering the story, so we should cover it, too.

The news editor told me to go ahead and write it up—which I finished doing just a few minutes ago!

How do you know how much to write?

The more important a story is, the more space it can take up in the paper. Even then, stories can't be too long.

The news editor liked what I told her about the story, so she thought it deserved plenty of space. Most of the space would be taken up by a picture, however. Good pictures are really important in newspapers. Because television can show exciting film of events, newspapers have to work extra hard to show something special that people won't see on TV.

Luckily, the photographer snapped a wonderful picture of a whale with steam shooting out of its blowhole. Even if a TV camera filmed that happening, it wouldn't look as good as it does in a frozen image. Sometimes, things look better when they're not moving.

If the photograph hadn't been good, the story would probably not get as much space. For some stories, photos are not important. However, when you have a story about whales swimming into the bay, you need good pictures!

The photographer tells the news editor that he took a really great shot!

Stories in newspapers are measured in inches. When we hit a special key on our computers, it tells us how long our story is. The news editor told me to write about twelve inches on the whale story. This is about three hundred and fifty words. After all the hours we spent with the whales and all the people we spoke to, this wasn't very much space!

Because so much happens each day, and because there are so many stories trying to get into the paper, most stories have to be short. This means a journalist has to be extra skillful to get all the important information into the story.

How do you decide what is important?

When you write a news story, you have to decide what the reader needs to know to understand it. There is an old rule journalists use when writing news stories. It is called the "Who What When Where Why and How" rule. This means that when a reader reads a story, they have to know who was involved, what happened, when it happened, where it happened, why it happened, and how it happened.

It is good to get all of this into the first paragraph or two of the story. After that, you can develop the story by quoting the people you interviewed. "Quoting" is when you use a person's actual words in your story.

When you interview people, they usually say much more than you can include. You have to pick the quotes you really need to tell the story. You also have to be careful not to make it sound like the person is saying something he or she did not mean.

What happens to the story now?

As soon as I finished the story, I sent it to the news editor. She read it quickly, just to make sure I covered the story in the way we had discussed. You can always put new ideas into a story, but the news editor has to agree with them.

If the news editor thinks your story is missing something, she can ask you to add to it. This might mean going over your notes and putting in things you left out. Or you might have to make some phone calls to find out new information.

If the news editor thinks your story is not well-written, she can ask you to write it all over again. I'm glad to say this hasn't happened to me for a long time.

The news editor was happy with my whale story and sent it to one of the copy editors. The copy editor read my story very carefully.

What on earth is a copy editor?

Copy editors are some of the most important people in a newspaper, but not many people know about them.

Copy editors read the stories to make sure they read well. They correct any spelling mistakes or bad punctuation. Sometimes, they will rewrite part of a story to make it read better. This is helpful when a journalist has not had much time to write a story.

Sometimes, if there is not enough space for your story, parts of it can be cut out so that it fits the page. This is something the copy editor does. When copy editors need to cut stories, they must be careful not to change the meaning of the story. When they're not sure about the changes, they can check with the journalist—if there's time, that is.

At some newspapers, after the story has been copyedited, the copy editor will think of a headline for it and write a caption for the photograph. The story is then placed onto a page layout, which is a plan showing where the story will appear in the paper.

The most important stories of the day usually go on page 1 of the paper. My whale story is going on page 3, which is still pretty important.

In the old days, newspaper stories were written on paper with typewriters. Page layouts were worked out on large sheets of paper. Today, everything is done on computers. Even the photos are stored on computer. This means everything can be done faster and with fewer problems.

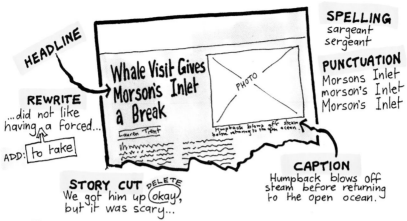

19

So how did the story turn out?

Here is my story about the whales:

The quiet fishing community of Morson's Inlet was disrupted yesterday when a pod of humpback whales swam in from the ocean. The whales, apparently confused by changing ocean currents, swam into the inlet at about six in the morning and remained until one in the afternoon.

Because of the size of the whales—which can weigh as much as forty tons—local police issued a safety warning, and instructed all fishing boats to remain moored

until the whales had left. Though they believed the chance of a whale deliberately capsizing a fishing boat was small, there was still the risk of an accident, and so it was best to wait for the whales to leave.

"These whales are powerful enough to knock over some of the smaller fishing boats we have here," said Sergeant Peter Moore of the Morson's Inlet Police. "We know that people rely on fishing for their livelihood, but we can't take the risk of someone getting hurt."

Though most residents agreed with the precaution, some did not like having to take a forced vacation.

"I've got to get out there and earn a living," said Jake Bapto, who has been fishing off Morson's Inlet for thirteen years. "Those whales may be big, but they're not as big as the mortgage I've got to pay off."

One person who was all in favor of the precaution was Frank Smedler, a resident of Morson's Inlet for twenty-four years. Ten years ago, Morson's Inlet had a similar visit by a pod of humpback whales. Mr. Smedler's small fishing boat, *Jewel Sea*,

was hit by one of the whales, and his son fell overboard.

"We got him up, but it was scary," Mr. Smedler said. "As far as I'm concerned, when the whales come here for a swim, they can have the place all to themselves."

It is still a mystery why the whales came into the inlet. Marine biologist Mary Weenis said it was possible that changing ocean currents caused by the El Niño effect may be to blame.

"Whales are creatures of habit, and when something they are used to is changed, they can get confused," she said.

How will the story look in the paper tomorrow?

A production editor is in charge of the way the pages in each section will look. You can ask the production editor to show you almost exactly how the story is going to look. Just remember to be polite!

This is how my whale story is shaping up.

Looks good, doesn't it?

NEWS

Whale Visit Gives Morson's Inlet a Holiday

Lauren Trent

Humpback whale blows off steam.

The quiet fishing community of Morson's Inlet was disrupted yesterday when a pod of humpback whales swam in from the ocean. The whales, apparently confused by changing ocean currents, swam into the inlet at about six in the morning and remained until one in the afternoon.

Because of the size of the whales – which can weigh as much as forty tonnes – local police issued a safety warning and instructed all fishing boats to remain moored until the whales had left. Though their belief believed the chance of a whale deliberately capsizing a fishing boat was small, there was still the risk of an accident, and so it was best to wait for the whales to leave.

"These whales are powerful enough to knock over some of the smaller fishing boats we have here," said Senior Sergeant Peter Moorie of the Morson's Inlet Police. "We know that people rely on fishing for their livelihood, but we can't take the risk of someone getting hurt."

Though most residents agreed with the precaution, some did not like having to take a forced holiday.

"I've got to get out there and earn a living," said Jake Bapto, who has been fishing off Morson's Inlet for thirteen years. "Those whales may be big, but they're not as big as the mortgage I've got to pay off."

One person who was all in favour of the precaution was Frank Smedler, a resident of Morson's Inlet for twenty-four years. Ten years ago, Morson's Inlet had a similar visit by a pod of humpback whales. Mr Smedler's small fishing boat, *Jewel Sea*, was hit by one of the whales and his son fell overboard.

"We got him up, but it was scary," Mr Smedler said. "As far as I'm concerned, when the whales come here for a swim, they can have the place all to themselves."

It is still a mystery why the whales came into the inlet. Marine biologist Mary Weenis said it was possible that changing ocean currents caused by the El Niño effect may be to blame.

"Whales are creatures of habit, and when something they are used to is changed they can get confused," she said.

Woman may hold key to disappearance

By Susan White

Police said yesterday it was possible that well-known clairvoyant Jasmine Jack could help locate the whereabouts of the infamous underworld figure Terrie Kracker.

Sources seem to indicate that Ms Kracker was last seen on the golf course during a seminar in Norville. Ms Cracker was well known for her love of the game of golf.

Staff became concerned when they realised that her bank accounts had not been touched, her car was in the driveway and nothing had been taken from the house, which was still locked and showed no signs of forced entry.

Jasmine Jack has been commissioned by Ms Cracker's assistant Ms Biskett to put her years of experience as a clairvoyant to work.

Jasmine Jack, when contacted has refused to comment except to say "She is trying to piece together some crumbs of evidence."

Do all the stories you write get printed?

No way! Even after a story has been put on the page, it still might not make it into the paper. There are a number of reasons this can happen.

Most newspapers rely on advertising to make money. Businesses buy space in newspapers to advertise their products and services. When pages are laid out, the copy editor and the production editor have some idea of how much space is going to be used for advertisements.

However, the amount of advertising space can change. If a company suddenly decides to place a big advertisement on a page, then stories that were going to go on that page have to make way for it. When this happens, a story may have to be shifted to another page. If another space can't be found, the story might have to be left out, or "dropped," from the paper. After all that work!

Another reason a story might not appear in the paper is because a more important story has to take its place. This happens quite often in big city newspapers. When an important story happens late in the day, it is called late-breaking news.

Late-breaking news can happen anywhere, at any time. A politician might resign, a famous person might die, or a big accident might happen. There might be an important announcement about a war. When late-breaking news happens, everybody has to work hard and fast to make room for the new story. Big stories that were on the front page might now be smaller stories on page 3. Some stories might have to be dropped. It doesn't mean there is anything wrong with the stories. There just isn't room for them.

It can be very exciting to be in a newspaper office when late-breaking news comes in. Everybody runs around, trying to get the big news story in.

What are the rules of being a journalist?

There are very strict rules you have to follow when you are a journalist. If you break any of the rules, you can be punished. You could even lose your job.

The most important thing is always to be fair, honest, and accurate when you write stories. This is because people believe what they read in newspapers. You have to report the whole truth, too. If you know something that is important to a story, you are not allowed to hide it. And you are not allowed to make things up!

You are not allowed to have a personal interest in a story. For instance, if you have a friend who is starting up a new business, you can't write a story just to help get that business started. You can't use a newspaper to do personal favors for people.

The rules apply to editors as well. Editors have to be fair and honest in the way they present stories. They also have to be fair and honest in the way they hire journalists. They are not supposed to give jobs to people just because they are friends or relatives. This would be unfair to all the other journalists.

For editors, the most important rule is to make sure the newspaper is independent. This means not letting people outside the newspaper tell the editor what to do. For instance, a company might try to stop a newspaper printing a story that makes the company look bad. It might threaten to stop advertising in the paper. A good newspaper would print the story anyway.

I'm glad to say none of this kind of thing ever happens at the newspaper I work for.

Sometimes I'm really in demand!

What happens if you get something wrong?

One of the most important things about being a journalist is that you have to get everything right. It is probably the most important part of the job. Making a mistake is very serious, but sometimes journalists do make mistakes.

Mistakes can happen for a number of reasons. A person who has been interviewed can be quoted incorrectly, or a journalist can accidentally get a fact wrong. Sometimes, a copy editor will change a story and cause a mistake.

When a mistake happens, the newspaper prints a correction. If someone complains that a mistake in the paper hurt or embarrassed him or her, the paper might print an apology. Newspapers take complaints seriously.

One of the biggest reasons mistakes happen is because of deadlines.

We made a mistake

On page 5 of yesterday's paper we wrongly referred to "Miss Primrose Beaurepaire" when her correct title is "Dr. Primrose." This mistake was made by a journalist. We apologize to Dr. Primrose.

What is a deadline?

A deadline is the time by which your story must be written. You have to allow time for the story to be checked and put on the page before it goes to the huge printing presses in the bottom of the building.

Newspapers are printed every night. The first edition is printed around midnight. There may be other editions printed a few hours later, with new stories and updates on late-breaking news. This means most stories have to be written by early in the evening.

Big stories go on big rolls of paper.

Suppose you are told that your deadline is seven o'clock in the evening, and you start writing your story at three o'clock in the afternoon. That's a lot of time for most stories.

But what if you start writing your story at half-past six in the evening? That's not a lot of time!

Sometimes, if the production editor knows a story is going to be late, the page can be held. If one page is being held for a late story, it can hold up the whole paper, so it must be important. Having a page held can give you a bit of extra time, but not much.

It's too late to stop the presses now.

The more time you have to write a story, the more careful you can be. You can double check things and call people back to make sure the facts and quotes you are going to use are correct.

Sometimes, a journalist can have more time to write a story, especially if it is a feature. Features are longer stories about important people, issues, and events. Feature writers can sometimes spend days— even weeks—writing a story. They are able to include more detail than is possible in a normal news story, so they require more time for research.

If you don't have much time to write a story, you can make mistakes, even though you don't mean to.

So, Lauren, what's your next story about?

I'm not sure yet. The whale story this morning came from a report on the radio. The next story could come from somewhere else. Story ideas can just come from an idea someone has about something. For instance, a journalist might see a person in a wheelchair having trouble getting into a store because of the steps. So the journalist might think about doing a story on how hard it is to move around if you are disabled.

Sometimes, ideas come from press releases. A press release is information that people send to newspapers to let them know that something is going to happen. Press releases are sent out by all kinds of organizations. Governments make many announcements by sending the media press releases. Companies launching new products also issue press releases. Every day, newspapers receive many more press releases than they can use. That's why news conferences are so important. The editors need to decide what is worth following up, and what isn't.

Another way to get story ideas is through contacts. Contacts are people you know who can suggest stories. They are usually people who know what's going on in particular public arenas. So you might have contacts in the government, on the police force, or in the courts. Sometimes, a contact will give you some information about a story that nobody else knows about. This is good, because it means you will be the first with the story.

Sometimes, a story idea will come from reading another newspaper. You'd be surprised how often that happens.

Is being a journalist a good job?

Being a journalist is an exciting job, because what you do one day can be very different from what you do the next. You get to meet interesting people and see interesting things that most people don't see, like whales swimming in the bay.

Probably the best thing about being a journalist is the people you work with. There are always interesting people to meet and talk to, especially in a newsroom as big as ours.

Journalists help each other out. If you're having trouble with a story, you can always ask another journalist to read over your story and tell you what he or she thinks. If you're having trouble getting started on a story, talking about it with other journalists can help.

Also, journalists make good friends. A newspaper only lasts a day, but having a journalist as a friend can last a lifetime!

Glossary

copy editor a person who reads newspaper stories before they are printed to check that they read well, don't contain any errors, and who sometimes writes a headline and photo caption for each story

El Niño an irregular warming of the southern Pacific Ocean surface that is linked with unusual global climate patterns that occur every few years; it causes far-reaching changes in weather, bringing dryness to some regions and heavy rainfall to others

press release information circulated to media by companies, organizations, or governments who want to announce and publicize some information or an event

production editor a person who is responsible for the way the pages of each section of the newspaper look

section editor a person who is in charge of one part of the newspaper, such as national news or sports

telephoto lens the lens used on a camera to produce a large, magnified image when photographing objects in the distance

Index